The Religion of Theosophy

By Bhagwan Das

Copyright © 2021 Lamp of Trismegistus. All rights reserved. No part of this publication may be reproduced or transmitted in any form or by any means, electronic or mechanical, including photocopying, recording, or by any information storage and retrieval system, without permission in writing from Lamp of Trismegistus. Reviewers may quote brief passages.

ISBN: 978-1-63118-565-6

Esoteric Classics

Other Books in this Series and Related Titles

Aurora of the Philosophers by Paracelsus (978-1-63118-507-6)

Clairvoyance and Psychic Abilities by A Besant &c (978-1-63118-403-1)

The Feminine Occult by various authors (978-1-63118-711-7)

Rosicrucian Rules, Secret Signs, Codes and Symbols by various (978-1-63118-488-8)

An Outline of Theosophy by C W Leadbeater (978-1-63118-452-9)

Paracelsus, the Four Elements and Their Spirits by M P Hall (978-1-63118-400-0)

Essays on Ancient Magic by Helena P Blavatsky (978-1-63118-535-9)

Essays on the Esoteric Tradition of Karma by A Besant &c (978-1-63118-426-0)

The Use of Evil by Annie Besant (978-1-63118-532-8)

The Alchemical Catechism of Paracelsus by Paracelsus (978-1-63118-513-7)

Alchemy in the Nineteenth Century by Helena P Blavatsky (978-1-63118-446-8)

Qabbalistic Teachings and the Tree of Life by M P Hall (978-1-63118-482-6)

The Historic, Mythic and Mystic Christ by Annie Besant (978–1–63118–533–5)

The Hidden Mysteries of Christianity by Annie Besant (978–1–63118–534–2)

History, Analysis and Secret Tradition of the Tarot by Hall &c (978-1-63118-445-1)

Crystal Vision Through Crystal Gazing by Frater Achad (978-1-63118-455-0)

The Golden Verses of Pythagoras: Five Translations (978-1-63118-479-6)

Arcane Formulas or Mental Alchemy by W W Atkinson (978-1-63118-459-8)

The Machinery of the Mind by Dion Fortune (978-1-63118-451-2)

The A E Waite Reader: A Selection of Occult Essays (978-1-63118-515-1)

The Leadbeater Reader: A Selection of Occult Essays (978-1-63118-483-3)

Audio versions are also available on Audible, Amazon and Apple

Other Books in this Series and Related Titles

The Spirit of Zoroastrianism by Henry S Olcott (978–1–63118–564–9)

The Brotherhood of Religions by Annie Besant (978–1–63118–563–2)

Fourth Book of Maccabees by Josephus (978-1-63118-562-5)

The Story of Ahikar by Ahiqar (978-1-63118-561-8)

Vision of the Spirit by C. Jinarajadasa (978-1-63118-560-1)

Occult Arts by William Q. Judge (978-1-63118-559-5)

Kali the Mother by Sister Nivedita (978-1-63118-558-8)

Love and Death by Sri Aurobindo (978–1–63118–557–1)

Times and Seasons Volume 1, Numbers 4-6 (978-1-63118-556-4)

Times and Seasons Volume 1, Numbers 1-3 (978-1-63118-555-7)

The Book of John Whitmer by John Whitmer (978-1-63118-554-0)

Interesting Account of Several Remarkable Visions (978-1-63118-553-3)

The Evening and Morning Star Volume 1, Numbers 11 & 12 (978-1-63118-552-6)

Private Diary of Joseph Smith 1832-1834 (978-1-63118-546-5)

An Address to All Believers in Christ Elder David Whitmer (978-1-63118-545-8)

A Manuscript on Far West by Reed Peck (978-1-63118-544-1)

The Story of Mormonism by James E Talmage (978-1-63118-543-4)

The Philosophy of Mormonism by James E Talmage (978-1-63118-542-7)

The Angel of the Prairies or A Dream of the Future (978-1-63118-541-0)

The Book of Abraham: Mormon History by George Reynolds (978-1-63118-540-3)

Pearl of Great Price by Joseph Smith (978-1-63118-539-7)

Audio versions are also available on Audible, Amazon and Apple

Table of Contents

Introduction…7

The Religion of Theosophy…9

INTRODUCTION

The word "esoteric" can be difficult to define. Esotericism in general can be seen less as a system of beliefs and more as a category, which encompasses numerous, different systems of beliefs. It's a bit of juxtaposition, since the word "esoteric" indicates something that few people know about, while the term itself broadly covers numerous philosophies, practices, areas of study and belief systems.

In a greater sense, Esotericism acts as a storehouse for secret knowledge, which is often considered ancient (by *tradition, if not by fact),* passed down from generation to generation, in private. At various times in history, simply possessing the knowledge of some of these subjects, was considered illegal and a jailable offence, if discovered. This usually included such general topics as Alchemy, Pharmacology, Qabalah, Hermeticism, Occultism, Ceremonial Magic, Astrology, Divination, Rosicrucianism and so on. Collectively, these areas of study were often referred to as the esoteric sciences.

Sometimes, the outer garment of a subject isn't esoteric, while what is hidden beneath it, is. As an example, Freemasonry isn't necessarily esoteric by nature (at *least not anymore),* but certain signs, passwords and handshakes given to the candidate during their initiation, are in fact, esoteric, in the sense that they are hidden from the general public.

Today, in the twenty-first century, such topics are readily available at bookstores across the country, and numerous mainsteam publishers offer beginners guides and coffee-table volumes on many of these subjects, intended for mass appeal. Books like *"The Secret"* have turned previously arcane topics into household knowledge. All that being the case, however, it isn't to say that there still aren't buried secrets to uncover, ancient wisdom being ignored and forgotten mysteries to be explored. In fact, it is often that we are only able to further our own studies by standing on the shoulders of these disappearing giants.

Lamp of Trismegistus is doing its part to help preserve humanity's esoteric history by making some of these classics available to those students who are seeking to unearth the knowledge of these ancient colossi.

So, be sure to check other titles from our *Esoteric Classics* series, as well as our *Occult Fiction, Theosophical Classics, Foundations of Freemasonry Series, Supernatural Fiction, Paranormal Research Series, Studies in Buddhism* and our *Christian Apocrypha Series.* You can also download the audio versions of most of these titles from Amazon, Apple or Audible, for learning on the go.

THE RELIGION OF THEOSOPHY

The duty assigned to me, in this Convention of Religions, and appropriately at its very end, is to place before you a brief statement of the Religion of Theosophy - which includes and sums up all religions.

We have met together under the aegis of the British Government today - representatives of many creeds and races; and our common medium of communication is the English language. This language - the language of a people who, in the modern world, have approached nearest perhaps of all nations, though very far from attaining yet, to that due balancing of the intellectual, the militant and the industrial [or Brahmana, Kshattriya and Vaishya] vocations, types and aspects of individual men and collective Society which makes a healthy and happy social organization - this language is spoken today by about 125 millions of human beings, and is understood by probably 25 millions more in all parts of the world, especially amongst the thoughtful and educated of all nations. Hence it is perhaps the best medium for the spreading of ideas over the wide surface of the earth at the present time. Hence, apparently were the epoch-making works of Madame H. P. Blavatsky, herself a Russian by birth, written in the English language. And hence I shall discuss the Religion of Theosophy in the terms of that rich- worded language, which is likely to be true and full of meaning .in the etymologies of all its important words, because developed by the guiding genius and containing within it the spirit of a people who, being the product of the mixing's of almost all the sub-divisions of the Aryan Race, are perhaps the most many- sided in mind, and who are comparatively well-balanced and just and righteous in themselves, on the whole. With the help of that language I shall endeavor to show to you, though all too cursorily, that the Religion of Theosophy is that Universal Religion which runs through all special religions and includes them all, even as the solar energy runs through all the endless forms and marvelous manifestations of heat, light, electricity, magnetism, X-rays, N-rays, etc., on our earth, and includes them all; even as the genus runs through and encloses all individuals; even as humanity is present in and enfolds all human beings however much any of them may regard themselves as separate, and strive to cut themselves off from any others.

The word Religion, by Latin derivation, means something which binds. And Religion is essentially that something which binds together the hearts of all men, without distinction of race, creed, caste, color, or sex; binds them all to each other with the golden thread of Universal Brotherhood; binds them to the heart of that Universal God who is the very Principle of Life, of Consciousness, of Being, in every thing and all things. It is that which binds the hearts of men to all ideals; which makes them *believe* in the now non-existent future; which compels them to work for the good of distant generations yet unborn, for the helping of the inhabitants of far countries never visited, for the realization of aims in a far-off age and place not at all visible to the fleshly eye of the present worker. It is that which makes the unbeliever by profession an unconscious believer by action, despite himself and despite all logic and consistency. All effort, all aspiration, for the distant, the future, the unknown — be the striving political or industrial, social or scientific, artistic or philanthropic, or even personal and selfish — is essentially religious. In all such striving, the element of the hope of success, of the faith in one's possibilities, of the belief in the continuance of the present into the future — be that future an hour distant or a million years — is the element of true Religion. It is the conscious or unconscious recognition of the fact that the spirit of man extends beyond the present moment, extends from the past through the present into the future, and that if it extends even a moment before and a moment after, then and therefore, for the same reason, whatever it be, it necessarily extends immortally throughout the eternity of time and the infinity of space, and embraces all things and beings, however much the bodies of men conflict and perish.

Wherever we have a *common feeling*, wherever we have *esprit de corps* however narrow, there we have the very *spirit* of Religion though restricted, there we have, however limited, the manifestation of the Unity of the Self, the Supreme Spirit, which alone binds together many selves into one, and makes of disjointed parts an organic whole.

The connotation of the Sanskrit word Dharma is the same:

"That which sustains and upholds all the worlds, that which maintains itself, that which is held close and fast by the wise and the virtuous, that which binds and holds together all the children of the Universal God, that which is the Supreme Spirit Itself" — that is Dharma."

Sympathy, fellow-feeling, love, the sensing of common Self of all in all — which is the one bond that binds and holds together individuals, families, tribes, nations, races, even as hate is the one sharp-edged instrument that sunders and scatters them apart — this love of all living things is of the very essence of Religion. Such Universal Love is the first and the last manifestation of God, the Universal and Immortal Self. It is this which triumphs eternally over Death and Hate and Evil. All association, all co-operation of any kind, within whatsoever limits, is the product of this Fellow-feeling, this Common-feeling, this One-feeling.

The Hindu seeks to regenerate and aggrandize the Hindu people. The Muslim labors for the cause of Pan-Islamism. The Christian strives to maintain undiminished the supremacy of the Christian nations. The member of the Hebrew race thinks only of the children of Israel and longs to restore the departed glories of Zion. The Buddhist, the Jain, the Sikh, the Parsi, each works for the people who bear the name of his religion. The same is the case with countries and nationalities. The Englishman, the German, the Frenchman, the American, the Russian, the Japanese, each feels surges of pride and satisfaction in thinking of the great deeds recorded in the history of his particular nation, but not so of any other.

Why is this so? Why is it that simply because I am named a Hindu in this present life, another person also bearing the name of Hindu, who lives two thousand miles away from me, near Cape Comorin or Peshawar, and whom I have never seen and never am likely to see, excites my concern in his troubles more readily, more deeply, more sincerely, than my brother of Islam or Christianity who is my next-door neighbor, and with whom I am brought into contact daily in various ways? Why should I take far more trouble to provide for the well-being of my great-great-grandson whom I shall never see, than for the comfort of this my neighbor but belonging to another creed? What solid and substantial reason can be given for such doings? Is it not a mere sentiment, an illusory feeling, an empty name, an airy nothing, a mere imagination and self-imposed hallucination — that my interests are the same as those of these unknown persons? He who runs may read that, in the great conflicts of religions, it is not the physical persons that are inimical primarily. For any one follower of any one religion can become a convert in a moment to any other, practically even if not nominally in one or two cases. It is the *Ideas* and *Ideals* that are in conflict. ' My *way of thinking and living* is the best and should be followed by all, and must prevail' — all mere imagination, idea, ideal. And yet these airy nothings, these mere sentiments and imaginations, cause wars and revolutions and overturn existing kingdoms, or discover and conquer new countries and build great civilizations and found new empires; depopulate and spread ruin over flourishing lands, or develop glorious new arts and sciences in them.

Therefore are these sentiments far more necessary to attend to than the so-called substantial things of life, even as the invisible air is more necessary to the living organism than solid food. They reign at the birth of life and at its decay and death also. They all, in their growing gradation of familism, parochialism, tribalism, provincialism, patriotism, nationalism, are but the manifestations of the feeling of the Common Self in larger and larger circles. And they are thus powerful in their operation, *because* they are all in growing degree embodiments of the Unity of the Omnipotent Spirit. And in the conflicts of religions, that religion will thrive most which best helps forward inclusiveness, and that religion must decay most which most fosters mutual separation and narrow-minded sectarianism and exclusiveness.

Whatsoever that Self identifies itself with, one interest or a thousand, one body or a thousand, whatsoever it makes *mine* by act of imagination, that becomes near and dear; whatever it dissociates itself from, whatever it regards as other, as foreign, as strange, that becomes distant and disagreeable. Brothers born of the same father and mother will slay each other for a trifle which may happen to come between and separate them. Utter strangers, from the ends of the world, will meet and marry as man and woman and become all in all to each other. Are not both phases the veriest tricks of the imagination, *mine* and *thine, mine* and not mine'? Verily, as the scriptures declare, nothing is dear except for the sake of the Self. And as the circumference of the individual self expands with growth of intellect and imagination, so more and more things and beings are enclosed within it. The man begins with identification of himself with (that is to say, love of) his own body, and goes on step by step to love of family, of townsfolk, of countrymen, of race, of fellow-religionists. Each one of these indicates one step in the growth and evolution of the soul. But the process is far from complete when it has arrived at the stage of patriotism and nationalism, Pan-Hinduism or pan-Islamism or pan-Christianism, or pan-whites, or pan-yellows, or pan-browns, or pan-blacks, or pan-reds. The synthesis of the Self is not yet perfect. The member of any one race, the follower of any one creed, sees and feels *himself* in the members of that race only, in the followers of that creed only. But a higher integration of these differentiated units is possible. It is possible to see and feel the Self in all men, whatsoever their creed or color. And if a common country, a common language, a common script, a common color of skin, a common idea, make such strong bonds, how much stronger the bond that a Common Self, a Common Life, should make between man and man! When that is done, when the Universal Spirit of all men is recognized and realized by all men, then will we have reached the stage of Humanism, the federation of all the nations. Of this stage the glorious Sufi sang:

> *Vedas, Avesta, Bible, Al-Quran,*
> *Temple, Pagoda, Church and Kaaba-stone —*
> *All these and more my heart can tolerate*
> *Since my Religion now is Love alone!*

A yet further reach remains — the state in which the soul recognizes its identity not only with all human life but with all lives whatever, above as well as below the human stage. Of that state of the soul it has been said that:

Seeking nothing, he gains all;
Foregoing self, the Universe grows " I ".

That is the ultimate stage of Religion, the culmination, by upward gradation, of all smaller degrees of fellow-feeling in the Great Feeling of the Common Life and Universal Consciousness in which all worlds and world-inhabitants live and move and have their being, the Great Feeling which different religions, speaking the same thing in different languages, have termed Moksha or Nirvana or Beatitude or Salvation or Meraj.

Such is the finality of all Religions. But we, who are met together in this Convention of Religions today are, I take it, striving to induce ourselves and our brothers to step into the penultimate stage, into that Humanism which will enfold within its patriarchal arms all smaller "isms" attached to special creeds, countries and races, and give equal share to each in the good things of life, equal place to each within its world-wide home, equal tolerance, nay, active affection, to each, letting each gain its goal and expand finally into the Ultimate along its own way in the distances of time.

Of great good augury, therefore, I believe, are such Conventions of Religions; the highest syntheses of all the many co-operative activities of the workers of today; the most hopeful sprouts of the seed of that all-inclusive Universal Brotherhood which is the very Religion of Theosophy, as embodied in the first and most important of the three objects of the Theosophical Society, *viz*. To form a nucleus of the Universal Brotherhood of Humanity, without distinction of race, creed, caste, color or sex.

And it needs no proof that this general principle of love and sympathy, of charity and humanity, of universal good-will and harmlessness, of aspiration and effort for the ever-growing welfare of all, is present in all religions.

But beside this general principle, there are some other features, more detailed aspects of that same principle, which also may be seen to be common to all religions and in which we may discern the real ground-plan of Comparative Religion.

Psychologists are agreed that the individualized consciousness has three aspects. Some call them intellect, feeling and volition. Some prefer the names thought, emotion and conation. Others call them cognition, desire and action. Others, imagination, will and self-assertion. Others, wisdom, will and activity. Others, wisdom, love and will, reversing the use of the words will and love, but meaning the same facts. Still others use other words. But there is a fairly general agreement as to the essential three facts or aspects involved: named in Samskrt jnanam, ichchha and kriya, by common consent of all *seers*. And as these are the aspects of Consciousness in its individualized form, so in its Universal form it shows forth the same as Omniscience, Omnipotence and Omnipresence. Men, as they show forth more of the one or the other of these aspects fall into one of three classes, men of thought, men of art, and men of action. And every Religion, being an embodiment of the feeling of that Common Consciousness, shows forth these three aspects also. It is true that, commonly, the word religion brings up the idea of a spiritual aspiration, a Godward emotion, a divine desire, a superphysical art; whereas metaphysics or philosophy may be said to represent the knowledge-side of the same, and concrete science the active industrial application; yet in its wider and fuller sense

Religion comprehends all these. In this sense, we may say that every religion tells its followers:

(a) What to think (or believe);

(b) What to desire (or feel);

(c) What to do. And Theosophy enables us to see that the essential teachings of every religion in respect of each of these vital questions, are practically the same.

> (a) Every religion includes within itself a body of doctrine more or less definitely formulated, a mass of knowledge more or less precisely expounded, relating to the whence, the whither, the how and the why of the visible and invisible worlds, and of the human and other life inhabiting these; and this part is its answer to the question: " What to think of all this world-process".
>
> (b) Every religion again has, as an integral part, a system of ethics or morality, which is its answer to the question: "What to feel or wish for or towards our fellow-creatures".
>
> (c) And finally every religion has a more or less elaborate code of sacraments and a general social polity, which is its answer to the question: "What to do to purify and elevate and make ever richer and more beautiful the individual as well as the aggregate physical and spiritual life of human beings".

These are the three ways, of Knowledge, of Devotion, and of Works, which belong to each and every religion and they are not *separable* from each other, any more than the three aspects of Consciousness. They are only *distinguishable* from one another, and all always necessarily co-exist and interweave, all making but One *Threefold* Path which must be trodden by every soul in its passage from the great deep to the great deep of the ineffable bliss and peace of the Divine Life. The dangers of trying to separate the three portions of this *triune* path and follow any one only and wholly abandon the other two are very great. Mere knowledge, reasoning, argument, science, unvivified by the living warmth of love, remains essentially incomplete and erroneous and leads ultimately to that deadly lack of interest, that stony coldness of heart, which is a taste of the isolation of Avichi, the motionless imprisonment of the writhing jinn in the sealed bottles of Solomon. Excessive Devotion, unbalanced, unadjusted, unguided by Reason, always leads, as history shows a thousand times, to unnatural perversions of emotion, to sex- corruption, hysterics, spiritism, unctuous cant, hypocrisy, nervous diseases of mind and body of all kinds; for love must move either upwards or downwards, and when, in the course of its spirals, it returns from the upward direction and cannot find the consecrated ways of wedlock in its fleshward journey, it perforce finds tortuous and evil ways for its expression, even as a healthy stream of water dammed back from its normal course between its natural banks, and not provided with healthier and more serviceable irrigation- channels, overflows the neighboring lands in harmful ways. Even so, Action uninspired by unselfish Love, unguided by Wisdom, becomes either aimless and meaningless mummery and superstition and ritualism, or positive vice and crime, a fever of restlessness and ruthless ambitions. Therefore all religions, which are at all complete show forth all three sides; they inspire Action with selfless Devotion, and guide both by Wisdom.

Under the sub-division of Knowledge, every religion teaches the existence of One Supreme Spirit, One Self-dependent all-pervading Life, binding together all beings in mutual relationships of duty and dependence. The nature of this Universal Spirit, hidden in the heart of every living thing, and yet also patently manifest in all things, is described in almost the same terms in the crowning teachings of every religion, the Vedanta of Hinduism, the Rahasya teachings of the Buddha and the Jina to their Arhat disciples, the Gnosis of the Christians, the Tasawwuf of Islam. Its conclusive evidence as well as closest and most primary manifestation is Consciousness, the immediate consciousness of every living being, Consciousness which proves all things else and which is proved by nothing else than itself. Of It has been declared: "Har che bini bi-dan ki mazhar-i-u-st", "Whatsoever thou beholdest know to be but a manifestation of That". Of It the Upanishats say: "Sarvam khalu idam Brahma", "Tat-twam asi", "Aham Brahm-asmi", "All this is Brahman", "Thou art That", "I am That also". Of It the great Teachers Shams Tabrez and Mansur declared: "Haq tu i" and "An-ul Haq", "Thou art God, the One Truth and Reality", and "I am That same". The great Islamic kalema of faith, "La ilah' Iillah'", There is no other God, no other true Being; or Creator, than the One God", is a declaration of the existence of the same One and Supreme Spirit, whose name is That (or rather, That-ness, in Sanskrit Tat or Tattvam, which, as a friend learned in Arabic said is the literal meaning of the word Allah). The Christian teaching also is that man is the living " temple of God " and that "I and my Father are one".

This universal belief in the existence of an Eternal Spirit pervading all things goes with the belief in the obvious appearance of an ever changing and passing material or objective world, in relation with which the Spirit puts on the triple aspect of Creator,

Preserver and Destroyer. Such a triplicity of mere *aspect* would not be denied even in Islam which, otherwise, in its insistence on the secondless Unity of the Supreme Spirit, and the repudiation and negation of all other-than-God, la-ilah, anatma, Not-Self, is as clear and emphatic as Advaita Vedanta.

Another belief common to all religions is the belief in other worlds than this; in other states of individual consciousness than the waking one; in other kinds of experience than those brought to us by the five physical senses. And most of us are beginning to realize today that within the infinite powers and possibilities of the Spirit, there might be as much variety in these invisible and superphysical worlds as in the visible one; or rather, indeed, far greater variety, for the known is infinitely less than the unknown, and yet, also, that which is visible to the eye of flesh every minute all around us is so very great a miracle that nothing else can possibly be greater ever and anywhere. The growth of forest-giants from tiny specks of seeds, the ever-blowing winds, the ocean-tides, the whole vast ball of the earth whirling round itself and round the sun in *empty* space with inconceivable velocity, the sun itself with all its planets rushing round some other vaster sun, the countless orbs of heaven shining as points of stronger light in an ocean of milder light — un-understandable yet plainly visible to the naked eye of flesh on every starlit night — all these are greater *miracles* than, or at least equal *miracles* with, endless grades and shades of subtlety and density of matter.

Yet another common item of belief is the existence of different grades of spiritual beings dwelling in and governing these different worlds, even as men and animals live in this, all within and under the Absolute Nature and Law and sway of the One Supreme Spirit which lives and moves in all, Devas of high and low degree,

Farohars, Elohim, Angels, Cherubs, Seraphs, Sprites, Fairies, Farishtas, Jinns, Paris, etc.— are the names, given by Hindu, Buddhist, Jain, Sikh, Parsi, Hebrew, Christian, Muslim, to these same spirits, some benevolent, some malevolent to humanity. All religions also believe, more or less clearly in special manifestations of the Supreme Principle of Consciousness, distinguishable within but not separable from the general manifestations of life, like a mountain amidst hills, like a sun amidst lesser lights. These special manifestations are stated in the scriptures of those religions, which deal with the subject at length, to be perpetually appearing, and in all kingdoms and on all planes of matter, below as well as above the human and the physical. In the human kingdom, the various religions call them by various names, Avataras, Aveshas, Amshas, Kalas, Buddhas, Jinas, Tirthankaras, Zardushtas, Sons of God, Rasuls, Messengers, Nabis, Prophets, Saints, Sages, Seers, Poets, Kavis, Rshis, Imams, Messiahs, Babs, Heroes, Geniuses, etc, etc. Each name has its own special significance of function and degree. The general principle underlying these special manifestations is that the Universal Self appears in them in an intenser form than in others, on special occasions, for special purposes of teaching, of adjusting and chastening of, and leading on by inspiring love. But the difference between the special and general manifestations is ever one of *degree* only, for it is literally true than *all* living things are the children of God, are Spirit of the same Spirit and flesh of the same flesh, are *Avataras, descents* of Spirit into Matter, are compounded of the self-same Spirit and Matter. Looked at thus, the fact of Avataras becomes divested of all sensational mystery and wonder-working and is seen to be only one of the facts of nature, and a fact which is much less overwhelmingly astonishing, if at all, than the daily marvels of sunrise and sunset. A homely illustration may perhaps make plain 'the mode of operation' of the Principle of Consciousness in such manifestations. In the case of a human individual, when a thorn pierces his foot, while the general vital-consciousness pervading and upholding the whole of his body is by no means wholly drawn away from all the other parts but continues to nourish them, yet there is a special concentration of it at the point where the thorn is rankling, and another corresponding concentration in the hand which, guided by (the Principle of) knowledge (Vishnu), travels to that point to remove the cause of the pain. Even so, in the life of a nation, a race, a group-soul, when Sin, Evil, Adharma, Prati-narayana, the spirit of Negation of the Self, Satan, Kama-Krodha, the Matter-ward tendency, Egoism, becomes excessive, then some soul embodying in an especial degree the principle of Virtue and Goodness and Love, Narayana, Vishnu, etc., appears to apply the remedy. Avataras come to show the way, to erect a standard, to set an example, to be imitated with effort and striving; they *do not* come in order to be blindly worshiped. Indeed, many have had occasion expressly to forbid such blind worship of themselves, as tending to retard the Realisation of the Great Self which is the end, Avataras being but means.

Finally all Religions teach, more or less distinctly, that the human soul, being a portion of the Divine Being, has emanated from it and will go back to it some day, after passing through various experiences of good and ill, virtues and joys, sins and sufferings, in various worlds. Detailed teachings on this periodical descent and re-ascent of Spirit, and the laws governing this evolution and involution of soul and body, through various stages and kingdoms of nature, in birth after birth, are to be found in the mystic traditions and teachings of every great religion, though sometimes preserved secret as *Ilm-i-sina,* in the *hearts* and memories of teachers and disciples, and not always published broadcast in the earlier days of the religion to the masses not yet ready to receive them for lack of the needed intellectual growth. But the main law governing all this evolution is accepted unanimously by all religions to be the Law of moral and psychical as well as physical Causation or Action and Re-action: As ye sow, thus shall ye reap; *Saza* and *Jaza* virtue is rewarded in the end, and vice punished; the wages of merit are joys, the wages of sin, suffering.

These, in very brief outline, may be said to be the chapters of faith common to that part of the book of any and every religion which deals with the question: "What to think?"

Another part thereof, dealing with the question: "What to feel?" is even more obviously common to all. All religions teach us to feel love for all — in the shape of reverence towards those who are older and greater than we, and in the highest degree for our own Inmost Spirit, the Supreme Self; in the shape of sympathy and affection for those who are equal to us; in the shape of tenderness and pity to those who are younger and weaker and smaller. All other virtues flow from these. And morality, the spirit of Loving Righteousness, is the very heart of Religion, as knowledge is its head, and performance of duty its limbs.

Without this spirit of Loving Righteousness, Religion were like a body without a heart, dead and putrefying and spreading corruption all round.

A high civilization, being but an aspect of a high religion, is made up of the same three factors. It is built up

> (a) of great stores of knowledge, of all kinds of science, physical and superphysical;

(b) of active industries and energetic enterprises; and even more vitally important than these;

(c) of high morals and purity in art. Genuine civilization and high culture might perhaps be reached with the help of scrupulous morality and fine (as distinguished from vile) art, which always subserves the highest and the noblest desires and emotions of love and devotion and patriotism and heroic courage, even without much science and without much mercantile and mechanical enterprise, as witness the classic days of Greece. But without these and even with much science and machinery, we can only have results like those- attending the sudden finding of a heavy nugget of gold by a rude miner, *viz* drunken carousals - and shootings. Without this inmost spirit of religion, without high-minded and spiritual earnestness and purity of character, without benevolence and charitableness and philanthropy, no nation can attain to genuine civilization, but at most only to that great display of brass and iron and silver and gold which history associates with *barbaric splendor,* be the forms taken those of helmet and bread-plate and lance and sword, or be they guns and cannon and armored trains and iron-bound men-of-war.

Indeed, the whole of history, the whole of political science, is but a perpetual illustration of the truths and principles of moral psychology. Pride goeth before a fall, in the nation as well as the individual, for the plain reason that arrogance estranges friends and creates enemies. Honesty is the best policy, for nations as well as individuals, because honesty is born of that sympathy which feels the Divine Life in all, and *therefore* instinctively wishes to do to another as it would be done by, and sympathy produces sympathy and converts enemies into friends. Frankness is the deepest diplomacy, for individuals as well as nations, because frankness inspires equal frankness and confidence in the long run, and where there is confidence there is no further room or need for that endeavor to circumvent, which is the currently understood meaning of the world diplomacy. They who promote strife between others, be they individuals or races, thinking to benefit themselves by the policy of *divide and rule,* generally find themselves unable later on to control the evil spirit of strife when once fully aroused, and come in for blows from both sides impartially; or find that that spirit so diligently invoked by them has ultimately invaded and taken lodgment within their own families and homes and created unquenchable internal dissensions. Hatred ceaseth never by hatred, between men as between nations, though it may possibly be driven underground temporarily by superior might and so compelled to bide its time — but it ceaseth wholly and only by love. Righteousness must prevail in the end between men and between nations, because it makes all loving to each other, and in such a condition of things only is permanence, and not in intrigues and diplomacies. Blessed are the peacemakers only, who studiously promote peace and love all round, amongst all, within their own homes, as well as within and between all other homes; only theirs is the kingdom of heaven, and not of heaven only but of this earth also, and permanently.

To take an illustration at random from the papers of the day and the country we are gathered in, the new Viceroy of India shows a just appreciation of the fact that a true and righteous psychology is the very foundation of all successful politics and beneficent administration, when he opens his first Council meeting with the expression of the "hope and belief that a *frank* expression of opinion will assist all to understand each other and *appreciate* one another's point of view", and *trusts* that the deliberations of the Council will be animated by a *spirit* of mutual concession and courtesy." And all other great and genuine and high-minded statesmen, all the world over, are also engaged with all their might in promoting *cordiality* and *removing distrust* between the nations, and between the classes within each nation; in restraining the smart and supercilious word which it is so pleasant to one's pride to utter, but which flings men and nations into lifelong bitterness and deadly feuds; and in encouraging the kindly and agreeable speech which makes men agree with each other. Truly what cometh out of the mouth is far more immediately important than what goeth in (though the latter cannot by any means be neglected), for the fate of nations as of men. And diligent *appreciation* of each other is far more useful, far more *paying*, in the common phrase, than depreciation. Thus only may the evil aspects of the spirit of unrest that is now moving over the whole face of the earth be allayed, and its good aspects brought to a just fruition.

Whatever, then, promotes moral and friendly relations between single individuals or between collective bodies of such is of the very essence of universal as well as special Religion, by whatever name it may be called; for it enables men to realize in life the Common Self of all.

Far more necessary than all else is it to promote this Fellow-feeling. This is why the Scriptures of all times and all nations teach continuously: "God is Love", "Love your neighbor as yourself", " Achieve humility of heart and earnest righteousness of spirit, and all things else will be added unto you". This is why they all say "Faith moves mountains", faith in each other, faith in the potency of co-operation, faith in ourselves, faith in the Divine Spirit surging in all. The nations, the races, the religions, that seek to promote unity or harmony as between their own constituents, sub-races and sects, while fostering contempt of and aggression against other nations, races, religions as such, indiscriminately — will *never* succeed in bringing about the wished-for harmony within their own limits. It is not possible to heat red-hot the half of an iron bar and keep the other half cool at the same time. We cannot foster evil emotions towards *foreigners* or *natives, whites,* or *blacks, browns,* or *yellows,* and at the same time permanently develop good emotions towards those within the same fold as ourselves. Universal Brotherhood and Religion must pervade all peoples before any one of them can be really happy.

The word Religion has indeed fallen on evil days. That noblest of all words, full of the sense of all- pervading, all-embracing Divine Life and Love, has been so befouled by associations of unhappy priestcraft and bigoted narrow-minded-ness and cruelty that many good men and true, full of the very spirit of Religion, shrink from acknowledging it even to themselves. Even so has that other noble word Loyalty, expressive of the manifestation of the spirit of Religion in action, been so befouled by self- seekers and false flatterers on the one hand and the arrogant claimers of blind obedience on the other, that the men most truly loyal, loyal to Truth, to Science, to Reason, to Art, loyal " to their King as to their conscience and to their conscience as to their King", are ashamed to avow and profess it. But because the gold has become bespattered with mud, we cannot throw it away. We must make it clean and bright as ever before. We must endeavor to restore Religion to its pristine purity and large-heartedness.

For to do so, and to spread this Religion of Love and Universal Brotherhood, is indeed to do the work of all sovereigns, all statesmen, all diplomatists and politicians and administrators, put together, and to do it far better than they are doing it today. For this is indeed to water the roots; while they are mostly only washing the leaves at best. And this is why the great Teachers and Founders of religions loom so much larger in the instinctive consciousness of humanity than the other kinds of workers, and are accorded divine honors, and regarded pre-eminently as incarnations of the Divine Spirit, special manifestations and messengers of the God of all nations and all religions, while even the greatest men of thought, men of art, and men of action are regarded as but minor characters in the drama of human history. The re-purification of the human race, time after time, from the gathered dust of decay and degeneracy, by the founding of a new religion — new in name and form and language only, but eternally old in underlying truth — by a new messenger of God, a more concentrated and more powerful manifestation of the Divine Consciousness — has always been followed by a great uprush of material progress and prosperity and the foundation of a new civilization, of revived and renascent and transformed thought, action and art — only because the religious Spirit of Love has made that co-operation possible without which great civilizations are not possible. The significance of the current conflicts between religions, *i.e.,* between various ideals of life, various ways of living, of thinking, feeling and behaving — is also but this, as said before, that by means of such conflicting ideals, the human racial consciousness is making experiments, and endeavoring to find out which is the best and the fittest for the time, place and circumstance; and the fittest, which will survive in the struggle, will necessarily be that which most promotes co-operation and love and sympathy, and most eradicates all exclusiveness and strife-making pride of too rigid caste and mutual dislike and contempt and separation.

We may see thus that the Vedanta, the Gnosis, the Tasawwuf — which teach that the Spirit in all is one and the same, and that *therefore* men should and ultimately must love each other — are not the vain visions of idle dreamers, but the most practical of all practical politics. And the answer of all religions to the question: "What to feel?" is: "Feel love for all and for each living creature, love in its many forms and modifications, each suited to its own corresponding situation in life; and behave to all and each accordingly".

And this is the second part of the book of every religion; and it is called Ethics.

The third part is the answer to the question "What to do?" It may be named the "Part of special Rites and Ceremonies and Sacraments, and special directions for the conduct of life, individual and collective."

These, in their detail, differ in the various religions, given to different peoples living in different countries, and differing more or less in their psycho-physical requirements. They differ as much, and in the same way, as clothes and foods differ with different lands and seasons and states of health and personal needs and individual temperaments. They are of no greater, but also of no less, consequence than these. *Some* clothes are necessary to the civilized man; but it is not absolutely necessary that they should be of any one particular cut and pattern; while a healthy body is absolutely necessary within all kinds of clothes. Even so, while Loving Wisdom is absolutely necessary for all, any particular sacrament or ceremonial or form of courtesy is not absolutely necessary for any one, though *some* is indispensable.

And so, even here, amidst the varying details of ritual, we may discern certain general principles underlying all schemes. Each Religion has a set of sacraments, some fewer, some more numerous, which may be divided into: (i) antenatal, (ii) post-natal, and (iii) post-mortem; connected with the three main events of life, *viz.,* birth, marriage and death. The purpose of all these is to purify and consecrate the grosser and subtler bodies, inhabited by the soul, in such a manner as to make its life here and hereafter higher, richer and nobler, and enable it to attain to ever greater and greater perfection and communion with God and Nature.

Each Religion has also some other rites and ceremonies, whereby communion with the inhabitants of other and invisible worlds may be obtained for various purposes.

Each also, to a greater or lesser extent, lays down some directions in the nature of laws of social and domestic polity, assigning various rights and duties, functions and vocations, to different men, of different temperaments, and in different stages of life. All this department of dharma duties, is essentially relative to time, place and circumstance.

This assignment of occupation and organization of society was, presumably, in most cases originally based explicitly or implicitly, on living and elastic data of psychical and physical characteristics, developed by spontaneous variation *as well as* careful selection and cultivation in accordance with the laws of that evolution which includes *both* heredity and origination of new species. But, in most cases also, the original idea has degenerated, by the lapse of time, from the old just balance and golden mean, into either the one extreme of a lifeless, ossified, birth ridden, "touch-and-I-die" caste or into the other extreme of chaos-making, organization-destroying lawlessness, and general leveling down of all by the willfulness of the least qualified.

But the restoration of the knowledge of essential truths, and of fellow-feeling, of Love and of Wisdom — of which restoration, Conventions like these give high assurance — will surely correct the errors of dual extremism in due course on this point also, and bring back again that well-balanced and well- planned social organization which is the golden mean between excessive regimentation on the one hand and disorder and mob-rule and lawlessness on the other, and whereby each human being will be given the fullest chance of developing the potentialities of good that are within, acquired by birth and heredity *or* by spontaneous variation, and of occupying thereafter his right place in the Social Household of the Human Family.

With this we may close our brief review of the three Parts of every religion and of the Universal Religion of Theosophy.

The three objects of the Theosophical Society correspond with these also.

To the Part of Knowledge, the jnana-kanda, corresponds the second object, *viz:* "To encourage the study of Comparative Religion, Philosophy and Science", whereby the truths common to all religions will be discovered. This is the object which is directly subserved by Conventions and Parliaments of Religions like this, where men of different faiths have the best opportunities of learning the common as well as the special features of the various creeds as presented by their most sympathetic and most liberal-minded exponents.

To the Part of Action, or Karma-Kanda, belongs the third object, *viz:* "To investigate the unexplained laws of nature and the powers latent in man" — whereby the bounds of knowledge will be pushed back further, communication established with what is now invisible and beyond reach, the meaning and purpose of the various systems of ritual become clear, and the life of the physical be rendered richer, purer, finer, by elevation to the superphysical.

To the Part of Love and Devotion or Bhakti-kanda, to which all high and real Art corresponds and is subservient, belongs that first and most important object, to spread of the conscious feeling of Universal Brotherhood, or in the words of the latest published statements: "To form the nucleus of the Universal Brotherhood of Humanity without distinction of race, creed, sex, caste or color."

It may be added here that the Theosophical Society — which now counts over 20,000 members, living in all parts of the world, under some 30 different governments (or if Colonial governments and States be counted separately, then over 100) and grouped into nearly 800 active Lodges in 18 different Sections — is a Society which "is composed of students, belonging to any religion in the world or to none, who are united by their approval of these three objects, by their wish to remove religious antagonisms, and to draw together men of good will, whatsoever their religious opinions, and by their desire to study religious truths and to share the results of their studies with others. Their bond of union is not the profession of a common belief, but a common search and aspiration for Truth. They hold that Truth should be sought by study, by reflection, by purity of life, by devotion to high ideals, and they regard Truth as a prize to be striven for, not as a dogma to be imposed by authority. They consider that belief should be the result of individual study or intuition and not its antecedent, and should rest on knowledge, not on assertion". So free is the Society on this point that many of its members keep a perfectly open mind and suspended judgment even with regard to the views that are now generally known to form part of what is called Theosophy. And in this sense Theosophy must be clearly distinguished from the Theosophical Society.

But the majority of the members believe that Theosophy is the body of truths which forms the basis of all religions and which cannot be claimed as the exclusive possession of any; that "it restores to the world the Science of the Spirit, teaching man to know the Spirit as himself, and the mind and body as his servants; and that it illuminates the Scriptures and doctrines of religions by unveiling their hidden meanings, and thus justifying them at the bar of intelligence, as they are ever justified in the eyes of intuition". It inspires Knowledge with Universal Love and Devotion and Brotherliness, it guides and steadily controls Love by Wisdom, and it brings these two together to their just fruit in benevolent Action.

The Council of the T. S. has in the press, even now, under the Editorship of Mrs. Annie Besant, the President of the T. S., a Universal Text-Book of Religion and Morals, modeled on the Text-Book of Hinduism published by the Central Hindu College of Benares, and therefore divided into three parts which may be distinguished in every complete religion. This paper may fittingly close with a quotation from its introduction.

"In modern days, the ease and swiftness of communication between the countries of the world no longer permits any religion to remain isolated and unaffected by its neighbors. Thought is more and more becoming international, cosmopolitan, and each religion is enriching itself by contact with others, giving and receiving fruitful ideas. Nor is this interchange confined wholly within the circle of living religions. Antiquarian and archaeological researches have brought to light pictorial, sculptural, and literary relics of religions now dead, belonging to vanished nations and perished civilizations; scholarship has gathered and classified these, and has established on an impregnable basis of facts the truth of the fundamental Unity of Religions. There are fundamental doctrines, symbols, rites, precepts, which are common to all, while the lesser variants are innumerable. It thus becomes possible to separate the essential from the non-essential, the permanent from the transitory, the universal from the local, and to find *quod semper, quod ubique, quod ab omnbus*. When this is done, we have remaining a fundamental religious and moral teaching which may fearlessly be given to the young, on the testimony of the religious consciousness of Humanity, as the expression of facts concerning God, Man, and the Universe, borne witness to by the elect of Humanity — the loftiest and purest human beings who have appeared in our Race — and mentioned also in living religions under the names of Vedanta, Rahasya, Gnosis, Tasawwuf, etc., as being capable of reverification by all who reach a certain spiritual stage of evolution . . . Nothing taught in history or science in our schools is endorsed by Teachers so august, and so far apart in time and space to the ordinary view; if we are justified in teaching anything to our children which they cannot verify for themselves, we are justified in teaching them these facts of religion and this moral law".

Conventions like this help on this work of the separating out of the essential from the non- essential, of the giving of fundamental religious and moral teaching to the young, and of showing to the world that all men are brothers and that religions unite and do not divide, if interpreted and followed as they ought to be.

And so we end where we began. There *is* a Universal Religion, and it is that which binds together the hearts of all men, and it is the Religion of Love which knows that the Self-same Spirit lives and moves in all, which therefore extends sympathy to all, and therefore also lives the life of duty, of self-denial and of continual self-sacrifice and helpfulness to others. And it is of this Universal Religion that the Buddha proclaimed the great mandate:

> Sound high the trumpet of that true Religion, Fling broad the banner of that large Religion, Live strenuously the life of that Religion, which binds the many progeny of God in one.

www.ingramcontent.com/pod-product-compliance
Lightning Source LLC
LaVergne TN
LVHW041503070426
835507LV00009B/793